BUILDING
THE CHRISTIAN HOME

A Marriage Enrichment Manual

John D. Schuetze

NORTHWESTERN PUBLISHING HOUSE
Milwaukee, Wisconsin

Cover illustration by Bill Scott.

Northwestern Publishing House
1250 N. 113th St., Milwaukee, WI 53226-3284
© 1994 by Northwestern Publishing House
Published 1994
Printed in the United States of America
ISBN 978-0-8100-0521-1

23 24 25 26 27 .28 29   19 18 17 16 15 14 13 12

TO MY GOD
who gave us these truths

TO MY FATHER
who passed them on to me

TO MY WIFE
with whom I live them

CONTENTS

INTRODUCTION

Unless the LORD builds the house,
its builders labor in vain.

Psalm 127:1

Good marriages don't just happen. They have to be built. And there's no better place to get advice than from the one who designed marriage in the first place.

In his Word God gives us the plan for a model marriage. He tells us how to build a beautiful home. Even though we are the ones who have to do the work, we are to let God serve as the foreman for this project.

With God directing the work, we are guaranteed success. We can be sure our labor won't be in vain. Instead we will have a building that is beautiful and a structure that is strong.

OUR MARRIAGE CONTRACT

(to be completed on wedding day)

On this special day we are making a promise to God and to each other. We promise to be guided by the counsel and direction God has given in his Word and reflect the love Christ has for his church. As a husband, I promise to love my wife as Christ loved the church. As a wife, I promise to submit to my husband as the church submits to Christ. We promise to be faithful to each other, cherish and support each other, and help each other in sickness and in health as long as we both shall live.

_____

Signature of Husband

_____

Signature of Wife

_____

Date

BUILDING
THE CHRISTIAN HOME

PART 1

Marriage
Enrichment
Sessions

SESSION 1:
THE
BLUEPRINT

Before we can build a home we need some blueprints. Blueprints give the contractor an idea what the final structure is to look like. In his Word the Lord gives us the blueprint for marriage. It's important that we study God's plan and follow it carefully. Only then can we build something that's beautiful—and something that will last.

1. **WHERE DID THE BLUEPRINT FOR MARRIAGE COME FROM?**

   Genesis 1:10—And God saw that it was *good*.

   Genesis 1:12—And God saw that it was *good*.

   Genesis 1:18—And God saw that it was *good*.

   Genesis 1:21—And God saw that it was *good*.

   Genesis 1:25—And God saw that it was *good*.

   Genesis 2:18-24—The Lord God said, "It is *not good* for the man to be alone. I will make a helper suitable for him."
   Now the LORD God had formed out of the ground all the beasts of the field and all the birds of the air. He brought them to the man to see what he would name them; and whatever the man

called each living creature, that was its name. So
the man gave names to all the livestock, the birds
of the air and all the beasts of the field.

But for Adam no suitable helper was found. So
the LORD God caused the man to fall into a deep
sleep; and while he was sleeping, he took one of
the man's ribs and closed up the place with flesh.
Then the LORD God made a woman from the rib
he had taken out of the man, and he brought her
to the man.

The man said,
"This is now bone of my bones
        and flesh of my flesh;
she shall be called 'woman,'
        for she was taken out of man."
For this reason a man will leave his father and
mother and be united to his wife, and they will
become one flesh.

Genesis 1:31—God saw all that he had made, and it
    was *very good*.

**When God laid the foundations of the world he also drew
up the blueprint for Christian marriage. As with the rest of
his world, God declared it to be very good.**

- - - - - - - - - - - - - - - - - -

2. WHAT IS GOD'S BLUEPRINT FOR CHRISTIAN MARRIAGE?

Matthew 19:4-6—"Haven't you read," he replied, "that
    at the beginning the Creator 'made them male and
    female,' and said, 'For this reason a man will leave
    his father and mother and be united to his wife,
    and the two will become one flesh'? So they are no
    longer two, but one."

Romans 7:2—For example, by law a married woman is bound to her husband as long as he is alive, but if her husband dies, she is released from the law of marriage.

Ephesians 5:25—Husbands, love your wives, just as Christ loved the church and gave himself up for her.

Christian marriage is the lifelong union of one man and one woman in an unconditional commitment of love.

3. **WHAT DOES THE BIBLE MEAN WHEN IT TELLS HUSBANDS AND WIVES TO LOVE EACH OTHER?**

1 Corinthians 13:4-7—Love is patient, love is kind. It does not envy, it does not boast, it is not proud. It is not rude, it is not self-seeking, it is not easily angered, it keeps no record of wrongs. Love does not delight in evil but rejoices with the truth. It always protects, always trusts, always hopes, always perseveres.

1 John 4:10—This is love: not that we loved God, but that he loved us and sent his Son as an atoning sacrifice for our sins.

God defines love as more of an action than an emotion. It involves what we do more than how we feel. God demonstrated such a love by sending Christ to be our Savior.

4. **WHO HAS THE RIGHT TO END A MARRIAGE?**

Matthew 19:6—"So they are no longer two, but one. Therefore what God has joined together, let man not separate."

God alone reserves the right to dissolve a marriage through death.

—————————————————————————

5. WAS DIVORCE A PART OF GOD'S BLUEPRINT FOR CHRISTIAN MARRIAGE?

Malachi 2:13-16—Another thing you do: You flood the LORD's altar with tears. You weep and wail because he no longer pays attention to your offerings or accepts them with pleasure from your hands. You ask, "Why?" It is because the LORD is acting as the witness between you and the wife of your youth, because you have broken faith with her, though she is your partner, the wife of your marriage covenant.

Has not the LORD made them one? In flesh and spirit they are his. And why one? Because he was seeking godly offspring. So guard yourself in your spirit, and do not break faith with the wife of your youth.

"I hate divorce," says the LORD God of Israel."

Matthew 19:9—"I tell you that anyone who divorces his wife, except for marital unfaithfulness, and marries another woman commits adultery."

1 Corinthians 7:15—But if the unbeliever leaves, let him do so. A believing man or woman is not bound in such circumstances; God has called us to live in peace.

Breaking the marriage bond is sin; divorce was not a part of God's blueprint for Christian marriage. Scripture reveals that marital unfaithfulness and malicious desertion break the marriage bond. In such cases the innocent partner who

14

was sinned against may obtain a divorce, which simply recognizes that the marriage bond has already been broken.

> Matthew 3:8—Produce fruit in keeping with repentance.

> John 8:11— . . . Jesus declared. "Go now and leave your life of sin."

Breaking the marriage bond is a serious sin regardless of the way our unbelieving society feels. The penitent sinner, however, finds forgiveness also for the sin of divorce through Jesus, who died to pay for all sins.

_ _ _ _ _ _ _ _ _ _ _ _ _ _ _ _

6. HOW DOES GOD BLESS THOSE WHO FOLLOW HIS BLUEPRINT FOR CHRISTIAN MARRIAGE?

> Genesis 2:18—The LORD God said, "It is not good for the man to be alone. I will make a helper suitable for him."

God blesses marriage with companionship.

> Genesis 2:24—For this reason a man will leave his father and mother and be united to his wife, and they will become one flesh.

God blesses marriage with sexual happiness.

> Genesis 1:28—God blessed them and said to them, "Be fruitful and increase in number."

God blesses marriage with children.

_ _ _ _ _ _ _ _ _ _ _ _ _ _ _ _

SUMMARY

God drew up the blueprint for Christian marriage at Creation. When he created man and woman he also instituted the basic social structure of marriage and the family. God intended that the marriage bond be a lifelong union—"till death parts us."

Divorce was never a part of God's blueprint for marriage. It is a serious sin which breaks the marriage bond and affects countless lives. Those who repent of this sin, however, find comfort and hope in Christ, who forgives all sins and mends broken lives. Therefore the Christian church will proclaim not only the law but also the gospel as it applies in each case.

The more we follow God's blueprint for marriage, the more we will enjoy the blessings of companionship, sexual happiness, and children.

PRAYER TO END THE SESSION

Gracious Father, we thank you for giving us the blueprint for Christian marriage. As with all of your creation, we, too, have to look at it and confess, "It is very good." Help us to make our marriage what you want it to be—a lifelong union of one man and one woman in an unconditional commitment of love. Lead us to work toward the goal of living an entire life of love with each other.

We also pray that you would bless our marriage. Bless us with a companionship that meets our various needs. Bless us with sexual happiness which can be found only in marriage. Bless us with the gift of children as you see fit. Help us always to follow the blueprint you gave us for Christian marriage. Amen.

FOR DISCUSSION:

1.   It is possible for people to fall in love at first sight.

2. Love involves having an exciting emotional feeling for someone else.

3. A marriage should be based on the commitment to love rather than on the feelings of love.

4. God selects one particular person for each of us to marry and will guide us to that person in some way.

5. One reason divorce is such a serious sin is because it affects the lives of so many people.

6. It is better for a couple to get a divorce than to be constantly fighting with each other.

7. Divorce is the unforgivable sin.

8. Since God forgives the sin of divorce, it isn't that serious when a person gets a divorce.

9. A person should never use forgiveness as an excuse for sinning.

10. A marriage is not complete without the blessing of children.

SESSION 2: THE BUILDING BLOCKS

To build a good house we need good materials. If we cut corners in order to save costs, chances are we'll pay for it later on. This applies also to marriage. We need high quality materials to build a strong marriage. In his Word the Lord gives us the building blocks for constructing a Christian marriage. The more we use these blocks and apply them to our lives, the more we will build a strong marriage.

1. **WHAT IS THE FOUNDATION FOR A CHRISTIAN MARRIAGE?**

   1 Corinthians 3:11—For no one can lay any foundation other than the one already laid, which is Jesus Christ.

Christ is the foundation for the Christian faith and life. He is also the foundation for a Christian marriage.

2. **WHAT ARE THE BUILDING BLOCKS FOR A CHRISTIAN MARRIAGE?**

   Ephesians 5:24—Now as the church submits to Christ, so also wives should submit to their husbands in everything.

Ephesians 5:25-28—Husbands, love your wives, just as Christ loved the church and gave himself up for her to make her holy, cleansing her by the washing with water through the word, and to present her to himself as a radiant church, without stain or wrinkle or any other blemish, but holy and blameless. In this same way, husbands ought to love their wives as their own bodies. He who loves his wife loves himself.

The main building block God gives for Christian marriage is love. This love is to reflect the relationship Christ has with his bride—the church.

Husbands are to love their wives as Christ loved the church:

- a self-sacrificing love

- an undeserved love

- a totally committed love

Wives are to submit to their husbands as the church submits to Christ. This submission, based on love, is to be:

- an unforced submission

- a trusting submission

- a totally committed submission

— — — — — — — — — — — — — — — —

3. WHAT HAPPENS TO THE FORMER TIES WHICH EXISTED BETWEEN PARENT AND CHILD?

Genesis 2:24—For this reason a man will leave his father and mother and be united to his wife, and they will become one flesh.

Marriage involves a "leaving" and a "cleaving." Man and woman leave the former ties of family, which take on a lesser degree of importance. They now cleave to each other and become one flesh, which is the closest and deepest human relationship.

> 1 Timothy 5:4—But if a widow has children or grand-children, these should learn first of all to put their religion into practice by caring for their own family and so repaying their parents and grandpar-ents, for this is pleasing to God.

> Proverbs 23:22—
> Listen to your father, who gave you life,
> and do not despise your mother
> when she is old.

The Lord wants children to honor, love, and care for parents, even in old age.

—————————————————————————

4. HOW DO THE ROLES GOD GAVE THE HUSBAND AND WIFE DIFFER?

> Ephesians 5:23—For the husband is the head of the wife as Christ is the head of the church, his body, of which he is the Savior.

God gave the husband the leadership role.

> Ephesians 5:22,24—Wives, submit to your husbands as to the Lord. Now as the church submits to Christ, so also wives should submit to their husbands in everything.

God gave the wife the submissive role.

—————————————————————————

5. ISN'T THE SUBMISSIVE ROLE AN INFERIOR ONE?

The submissive role may be an inferior one in certain kinds of relationships. This is not what God means, however, when he tells wives to submit to husbands. The different roles God gave husbands and wives were designed to complement rather than conflict with each other. The husband and wife are to be partners, not rivals.

THREE TYPES OF SUBMISSION*

FORCED SUBMISSION—This is the type of submission that occurs in the slave/master relationship. The master forces his slave to submit. He has no other choice. The master is clearly superior to the slave.

CARE SUBMISSION—Care submission occurs in a relationship when one requires obedience and submission from another, but in return cares for that person. The parent/child relationship is an example of care submission.

UNITY SUBMISSION—This is the type of submission God wants in the husband/wife relationship. Neither is superior, yet the wife submits to the husband as they cooperate and work toward unity. It is done for the welfare of the marital union.

--- --- --- --- --- --- --- --- ---

6. HOW, THEN, ARE THE HUSBAND AND WIFE TO USE THEIR GOD-GIVEN ROLES IN MARRIAGE?

Ephesians 5:21—Submit to one another out of reverence for Christ.

Matthew 20:28—"Just as the Son of Man did not come to be served, but to serve, and to give his life as a ransom for many."

---

*Stephen B. Clark, *Man and Woman in Christ* (Ann Arbor, Michigan: Servant Books, 1980). p. 41.

The husband and wife are to use their roles to serve God and each other. The husband is to be the SERVANT/LEADER. The wife is to be the SERVANT/HELPER.

---

7. **WHAT OTHER BUILDING BLOCKS DOES GOD GIVE FOR CHRISTIAN MARRIAGE?**

Ephesians 4:29—Do not let any unwholesome talk come out of your mouths, but only what is helpful for building others up according to their needs, that it may benefit those who listen.

Ephesians 4:25-27—Therefore each of you must put off falsehood and speak truthfully to his neighbor, for we are all members of one body. "In your anger do not sin": Do not let the sun go down while you are still angry, and do not give the devil a foothold.

Ephesians 4:15—[Speak] the truth in love.

Positive communication is an important building block for Christian marriage. Conflict is to be used to build up the relationship rather than tear it down.

Colossians 3:12-14—Therefore, as God's chosen people, holy and dearly loved, clothe yourselves with compassion, kindness, humility, gentleness and patience. Bear with each other and forgive whatever grievances you may have against one another. Forgive as the Lord forgave you. And over all these virtues put on love, which binds them all together in perfect unity.

God's Word gives many building blocks for Christian marriage. These include compassion, kindness, humility, gentleness, patience, and forgiveness.

22

Deuteronomy 24:5—If a man has recently married, he must not be sent to war or have any other duty laid on him. For one year he is to be free to stay at home and bring happiness to the wife he has married.

Another building block God gives us is time. Therefore the husband and wife are to give quality time to their relationship with each other.

--·--·--·--·--·--·--·--·--·--·--·--·--·--·--

SUMMARY

Christ is the foundation for a Christian marriage. The more a husband and wife strengthen their relationship with Christ, the more they will strengthen their relationship with each other.

The main building block for Christian marriage is love. This love is to model the love between Christ and his church. Even though both partners are equal before God, they have different roles in marriage. Both are to use their roles to serve God and each other.

Besides love, God's Word gives us many other building blocks that we are to use to build a strong marriage. The husband and wife are to give quality time to building a relationship that will last.

PRAYER TO END THE SESSION

Lord in heaven, we thank you for making Christ the foundation of your church. Through his perfect life and willing death he built us a home in heaven. This love not only saves us; it also serves as a model for Christian marriage. Husbands are to love their wives as Christ loved the church. Wives are to submit to their husbands as to the Lord.

Help us accept these roles as part of your will for our lives. And lead us to use these roles to serve you and our marriage partner. Draw us ever closer to you and your Word where you give us the building blocks for Christian marriage. Amen.

FOR DISCUSSION:

1. A marriage is hopeless if the husband or wife no longer loves the other.

2. A wife must do everything her husband tells her to do since she has promised to obey him.

3. Since the husband is the head of the family, he is to make all the decisions in the family.

4. The helper role is inferior to the leadership role.

5. The best thing to do when faced with marital difficulties is to consult with parents.

6. Our relationship with friends also changes after marriage.

7. Real communication means expressing all the thoughts and feelings one has.

8. When two people really love each other, they will naturally know what the other person needs and wants.

9. In a good marriage the husband and wife never have any conflicts with each other.

10. Since two become one in marriage, the husband and wife will always try to do things together.

SESSION 3:
THE
FINANCING

Few of us have enough money on hand to purchase a home. Therefore we have to arrange some form of financing. Money also plays a major role in building the Christian home, so it's important that the husband and wife manage their money wisely. Let's look at some guidelines God gives us in his Word, for he sets down some excellent principles for family finances.

1. **WHAT ATTITUDE DOES GOD WANT US TO HAVE REGARDING FINANCES?**

   2 Thessalonians 3:10—"If a man will not work, he shall not eat."

   1 Timothy 5:8—If anyone does not provide for his relatives, and especially for his immediate family, he has denied the faith and is worse than an unbeliever.

God expects us to work in order to meet the financial responsibilities he places before us.

   Matthew 6:25-34—"Therefore I tell you, do not worry about your life, what you will eat or drink; or about your body, what you will wear. Is not life more important than food, and the body more important than clothes? Look at the birds of the air; they do not sow or reap or store away in barns, and yet your heavenly Father feeds them. Are you not much more valuable than they? Who of you by worrying can add a single hour to his life?

"And why do you worry about clothes? See how the lilies of the field grow. They do not labor or spin. Yet I tell you that not even Solomon in all his splendor was dressed like one of these. If that is how God clothes the grass of the field, which is here today and tomorrow is thrown into the fire, will he not much more clothe you, O you of little faith? So do not worry, saying, 'What shall we eat?' or 'What shall we drink?' or 'What shall we wear?' For the pagans run after all these things, and your heavenly Father knows that you need them. But seek first his kingdom and his righteousness, and all these things will be given to you as well. Therefore do not worry about tomorrow, for tomorrow will worry about itself. Each day has enough trouble of its own."

God wants us to be concerned about financial matters, but not to worry about them. We are to trust that God will provide what we need in life.

Psalm 24:1—
> The earth is the LORD's, and
>   everything in it.

Matthew 25:14—"Again, [the kingdom of heaven] will be like a man going on a journey, who called his servants and entrusted his property to them."

We are to remember that we are only managers of the wealth we have. Everything really belongs to God.

2. HOW ARE WE TO MANAGE THE WEALTH GOD ENTRUSTS TO US?

Luke 12:48—From everyone who has been given much, much will be demanded; and from the one who has been entrusted with much, much more will be asked.

God expects us to be wise and faithful managers of the blessings he gives us.

— · — · — · — · — · — · — · — · — · — · — · — · —

3. WHAT DOES IT MEAN TO BE A WISE AND FAITHFUL MANAGER OF GOD'S BLESSINGS?

Luke 12:15-21—Then he said to them, "Watch out! Be on your guard against all kinds of greed; a man's life does not consist in the abundance of his possessions."

And he told them this parable: "The ground of a certain rich man produced a good crop. He thought to himself, 'What shall I do? I have no place to store my crops.'

"Then he said, 'This is what I'll do. I will tear down my barns and build bigger ones, and there I will store all my grain and my goods. And I'll say to myself, "You have plenty of good things laid up for many years. Take life easy; eat, drink and be merry." '

"But God said to him, 'You fool! This very night your life will be demanded from you. Then who will get what you have prepared for yourself?'

"This is how it will be with anyone who stores up things for himself but is not rich toward God."

As wise and faithful managers we will remember that our most important treasure is in heaven. We will also realize

that we are not to selfishly store away our material wealth for ourselves. Rather we are to freely distribute our blessings to meet the responsibilities God places before us.

————————————————————

4. HOW ARE WE TO DISTRIBUTE THE WEALTH GOD PLACES INTO OUR CARE?

Proverbs 3:9—
> Honor the LORD with your wealth,
>> with the firstfruits of all your crops.

We distribute our firstfruits to honor God and carry out his work.

1 Timothy 5:8—If anyone does not provide for his relatives, and especially his immediate family, he has denied the faith and is worse than an unbeliever.

We distribute some money to meet our needs and the needs of our family.

Ephesians 4:28—He who has been stealing must steal no longer, but must work, doing something useful with his own hands, that he may have something to share with those in need.

We distribute some money to help those in need.

Romans 13:6,7—This is also why you pay taxes, for the authorities are God's servants, who give their full time to governing. Give everyone what you owe him: If you owe taxes, pay taxes; if revenue, then revenue; if respect, then respect; if honor, then honor.

We distribute some money by paying taxes to support the government.

> Luke 5:16—But Jesus often withdrew to lonely places and prayed.

We distribute some money for rest and relaxation.

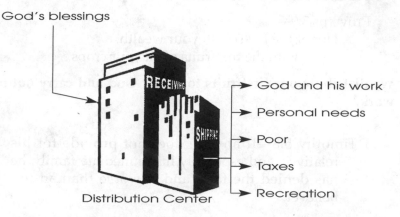

God's blessings

God and his work

Personal needs

Poor

Taxes

Distribution Center

Recreation

As Christian managers we are not to be storehouses for wealth but rather distribution centers for God's blessings.

5. WHY WILL WE WANT TO BE WISE AND FAITHFUL MANAGERS OF GOD'S BLESSINGS?

> 2 Corinthians 5:14—For Christ's love compels us, because we are convinced that one died for all, and therefore all died.

> 2 Corinthians 8:9—For you know the grace of our Lord Jesus Christ, that though he was rich, yet for your sakes he became poor, so that you through his poverty might become rich.

We want to be wise and faithful managers to show our love for Christ and our appreciation for what he has done for us.

6. WHAT WARNINGS DOES GOD GIVE REGARDING FINANCES AND MATERIAL WEALTH?

1 Timothy 6:6-10—But godliness with contentment is great gain. For we brought nothing into the world, and we can take nothing out of it. But if we have food and clothing, we will be content with that. People who want to get rich fall into temptation and a trap and into many foolish and harmful desires that plunge men into ruin and destruction. For the love of money is a root of all kinds of evil. Some people, eager for money, have wandered from the faith and pierced themselves with many griefs.

Hebrews 13:5,6—Keep your lives free from the love of money and be content with what you have, because God has said,
"Never will I leave you;
never will I forsake you."

So we say with confidence,
"The Lord is my helper; I will not be afraid.
What can man do to me?"

God warns us against selfishness and greed which can destroy our lives as well as our souls. Instead we are to be happy and content with the blessings God provides, recognizing they are generous gifts from his gracious hand.

Ecclesiastes 5:18-20—Then I realized that it is good and proper for a man to eat and drink, and to find satisfaction in his toilsome labor under the sun during the few days of life God has given him—for this is his lot. Moreover, when God gives any man wealth and possessions, and enables him to enjoy them, to accept his lot and be happy in his work—this is a gift of God. He seldom reflects on the days of his life, because God keeps him occupied with gladness of heart.

Psalm 127:2—
In vain you rise early
and stay up late,
toiling for food to eat—
for he grants sleep to those he loves.

God wants us to enjoy our work but he also expects us to manage our time wisely. We are to take time to serve God and each other.

SUMMARY

As we build a Christian home we need to be wise and faithful managers of the wealth God gives us. This will lead us to budget carefully so that all financial responsibilities are met, without needless worry and frustration. We are also to trust that God will care for us and to be content with the blessings he provides.

Besides managing our money, God also expects us to manage our time wisely. A good marriage doesn't just happen—it takes work. Only when we give plenty of quality time to the marriage relationship can we hope to build a strong home.

PRAYER TO END THE SESSION

Lord God, we thank you for all the blessings you give us in life. In your grace and love you provide more than we need. Please help us to be wise and faithful managers of these blessings. Keep greed and selfishness from gripping our hearts, and replace them with trust. You have promised to care for us, and we know you keep your promises. We have Christ's suffering and death on the cross as clear proof of this. Through Christ you forgive our sins and give us the gift of eternal life. When it comes to our earthly possessions, give us a strong trust. And give us wisdom so that we might use our money and time to your glory. Amen.

FOR DISCUSSION:

1. God doesn't want us to be concerned about finances.

2. Finances can cause a great deal of frustration in the home.

3. A person may have to miss church on Sunday in order to work and provide for the needs of the family.

4. It is more important to provide for the needs of the family than it is to give money to the church.

5. A Christian is to give all he has to the Lord.

6. A marriage that is financially stable will probably be a lasting marriage.

7. A marriage is usually hectic in the early years because the husband and wife are struggling to get ahead. Later on things begin to settle down.

8. Many marriages fail because either the husband or wife is too busy to meet the needs of the other.

9. Families have less time today than they did years ago.

10. It is just as important to manage our time wisely as it is to manage our money wisely.

SESSION 4:
THE
NEW
ADDITION

As time goes on, we may outgrow our house. We may need more space. To solve this problem we might build an addition. Like the rest of the house, this new addition also takes careful planning. This is even more true when that new addition is a child. This is the next thing we want to consider as we work at building the Christian home. We want to see what advice the Master Architect gives in planning for the new addition—the birth of a child.

1. **WHAT DOES GOD SAY ABOUT ADDING AN ADDITION TO THE HOME?**

   Psalm 127:3—
   > Sons are a heritage from the LORD,
   >   children a reward from him.

   1 Samuel 1:5,19,20—[The example of Hannah, the mother of Samuel] The LORD had closed her womb . . . and the LORD remembered her. So in the course of time Hannah conceived and gave birth to a son.

   Children are a blessing from God. Ultimately it is the Lord who gives or withholds this blessing.

   – – – – – – – – – – – – – – –

2. DOES THE BIBLE OFFER ANY ADVICE CONCERN-ING BIRTH CONTROL?

Genesis 1:28—God blessed them and said to them, "Be fruitful and increase in number."

God blessed the husband-wife relationship with the ability to bring children into the world.

1 Peter 3:7—Husbands, in the same way be considerate as you live with your wives, and treat them with respect as the weaker partner and as heirs with you of the gracious gift of life, so that nothing will hinder your prayers.

The husband is to be concerned about the mental as well as the physical health of his wife.

Hebrews 13:5,6—Keep your lives free from the love of money and be content with what you have, because God has said,
"Never will I leave you;
never will I forsake you."

So we say with confidence,
"The Lord is my helper; I will not be afraid.
What can man do to me?"

James 4:13-15—Now listen, you who say, "Today or to-morrow we will go to this or that city, spend a year there, carry on business and make money." Why, you do not even know what will happen to-morrow. What is your life? You are a mist that appears for a little while and then vanishes. Instead, you ought to say, "If it is the Lord's will, we will live and do this or that."

Selfishness or greedy desire for a higher standard of living or personal advancement are not to enter into family planning. We do not control the future, but let it in God's caring hands.

----

3. WHAT DOES GOD SAY ABOUT THE SEXUAL LIFE OF THE MARRIED COUPLE?

> Genesis 1:27—So God created man in his own image,
>   in the image of God he created him;
>   male and female he created them.

God created man and woman as sexual beings with sexual desires.

> Genesis 2:24—For this reason a man will leave his father and mother and be united to his wife, and they will become one flesh.

> 1 Corinthians 7:2-4—But since there is so much immorality, each man should have his own wife, and each woman her own husband. The husband should fulfill his marital duty to his wife, and likewise the wife to her husband. The wife's body does not belong to her alone but also to her husband. In the same way, the husband's body does not belong to him alone but also to his wife.

God provides the opportunities to fulfill the sexual desires in marriage. This is to be done in a self-giving rather than a self-gratifying manner.

> 1 Corinthians 7:5—Do not deprive each other except by mutual consent and for a time, so that you may devote yourselves to prayer. Then come together

again so that Satan will not tempt you because of your lack of self-control.

The marital couple is to abstain from sexual intercourse only by mutual consent and for a limited time.

> Hebrews 13:4—Marriage should be honored by all, and the marriage bed kept pure, for God will judge the adulterer and all the sexually immoral.

Sexual intercourse is to be enjoyed only by men and women who are married to each other. All sexual activity outside of marriage is sinful.

— · — · — · — · — · — · — · — · — · — · — · —

4. **HOW SHOULD THE CHRISTIAN FAMILY VIEW ABORTION?**

> Psalm 139:13-18—
> For you created my inmost being;
>   you knit me together in my mother's womb.
> I praise you because I am fearfully and
>   wonderfully made;
>   your works are wonderful,
>   I know that full well.
> My frame was not hidden from you
>   when I was made in the secret place.
> When I was woven together in the depths
>   of the earth,
>   your eyes saw my unformed body.
> All the days ordained for me
>   were written in your book
>   before one of them came to be.
> How precious to me are your thoughts, O God!
>   How vast is the sum of them!
> Were I to count them,
>   they would outnumber the grains of sand.

Scripture teaches that life begins at conception.

> Mark 10:14—Jesus . . . said to them, "Let the little children come to me, and do not hinder them, for the kingdom of God belongs to such as these."

> Matthew 25:40—"The King will reply, 'I tell you the truth, whatever you did for one of the least of these brothers of mine, you did for me.'"

The Christian couple will value and protect all human life, including the life of the unborn.

—————————————————————————

5. WHAT RESPONSIBILITIES DOES THE LORD GIVE CHRISTIAN PARENTS?

> Proverbs 22:6—
> Train a child in the way he should go,
>   and when he is old he will not turn from it.

> Colossians 3:21—Fathers, do not embitter your children, or they will become discouraged.

The father and mother are to exercise parental discipline over their children. This discipline should be carried out in love so that the child does not become bitter or discouraged.

—————————————————————————

SUMMARY

Even though the Christian couple can plan for a new addition, children are a blessing that God gives in his time. The Christian couple will gladly receive children and care for their needs and apply loving discipline when needed.

The blessing of sexual happiness was given to man and woman at Creation. Because of sin, however, man perverts this gift and misuses it. In marriage, God provides the couple with sexual intercourse not only as a means to bring children into the world, but also as a way to fulfill the sexual desire and express love and unity. This gift is not to be used as a bribe or a means of getting even. God clearly points out that all sexual activity outside of marriage is sinful.

PRAYER TO END THE SESSION

Father in heaven, we thank you for making us sexual beings and giving us the gift of sexual happiness. Forgive us for the times we have abused this gift either by our thoughts or our actions. Help us to use it in a way that is pleasing to you.

We also praise you for the ability to have children which flows from the sexual union. Lead us to value all life, including the life of the unborn. Give us wisdom to raise any new addition you may choose to give us as your child and an heir of eternal life. We offer this prayer because we are your children and you are our Father, through Jesus Christ. Amen.

FOR DISCUSSION:

1. Before getting married, each couple should decide how many children they plan to have.

2. It is wrong to practice any form of birth control.

3. Since children are a great financial responsibility, couples should wait until they are financially stable before having children.

4. A marriage in which God withholds the blessing of children is less than a complete marriage.

5. If two people love each other and plan to get married, it is okay for them to sleep together.

6. It is unwise for a husband and wife to discuss sex.

7. If the sexual life of a married couple is healthy, the rest of the relationship will be healthy as well.

8. The problem of abortion would be solved if the government made it illegal.

9. Abortion is wrong except in cases of rape and incest.

10. Balancing love and control is a key to Christian discipline of children.

SESSION 5: THE MAINTENANCE

Building a new house is only the beginning. After we move in we need to give it regular care and upkeep. The Christian home is no different. It also needs to be maintained so that the family not only stays strong spiritually but also grows in the faith.

1. **WHAT OTHER "MARRIAGE" DOES THE CHRISTIAN COUPLE NEED TO MAINTAIN?**

    Hosea 2:16,19,20—
    "In that day," declares the LORD,
        "you will call me 'my husband';
        you will no longer call me 'my master.'
    I will betroth you to me forever;
        I will betroth you in righteousness
            and justice,
        in love and compassion.
    I will betroth you in faithfulness,
        and you will acknowledge the LORD."

    As members of God's church we are "married" to Christ. He is the bridegroom; we are his bride.

    ----

2. WHAT DID JESUS DO FOR US, HIS BRIDE?

Ephesians 5:25-27—Christ loved the church and gave himself up for her to make her holy, cleansing her by the washing with water through the word, and to present her to himself as a radiant church, without stain or wrinkle or any other blemish, but holy and blameless.

Isaiah 61:10—I delight greatly in the LORD;
     my soul rejoices in my God.
For he has clothed me with garments of salvation
     and arrayed me in a robe of righteousness,
as a bridegroom adorns his head like a priest,
     and as a bride adorns herself
          with her jewels.

Revelation 19:7—
"Let us rejoice and be glad
     and give him glory!
For the wedding of the Lamb has come,
     and his bride has made herself ready."

As our bridegroom, Christ lived and died for us, his bride. We can now look forward to the eternal wedding feast of heaven.

_ . _ . _ . _ . _ . _ . _ . _ . _ . _ . _ . _ . _ . _ . _ .

3. HOW CAN WE SHOW LOVE TO OUR HEAVENLY BRIDEGROOM?

1 Corinthians 10:31—So whether you eat or drink or whatever you do, do it all for the glory of God.

Our whole life is to be a worship service to God. Everything we do is to be done to his glory.

Colossians 3:16—Let the word of Christ dwell in you

43

richly as you teach and admonish one another with all wisdom, and as you sing psalms, hymns and spiritual songs with gratitude in your hearts to God.

Romans 12:1,4-8—Therefore, I urge you, brothers, in view of God's mercy, to offer your bodies as living sacrifices, holy and pleasing to God—this is your spiritual act of worship.

Just as each of us has one body with many members, and these members do not all have the same function, so in Christ we who are many form one body, and each member belongs to all the others. We have different gifts, according to the grace given us. If a man's gift is prophesying, let him use it in proportion to his faith. If it is serving, let him serve; if it is teaching, let him teach; if it is encouraging, let him encourage; if it is contributing to the needs of others, let him give generously; if it is leadership, let him govern diligently; if it is showing mercy, let him do it cheerfully.

The Lord also asks us to set aside specific time for worshiping and serving him in the Christian congregation, as well as time for spiritual growth.

----

4. WHAT SPECIFIC TIME SHOULD BE SET ASIDE FOR THE LORD?

Hebrews 10:25—Let us not give up meeting together, as some are in the habit of doing, but let us encourage one another—and all the more as you see the Day approaching.

The Lord asks Christians to gather for worship. We do this through regular attendance in God's house.

44

Deuteronomy 6:5-9—Love the LORD your God with all
your heart and with all your soul and with all
your strength. These commandments that I give
you today are to be upon your hearts. Impress
them on your children. Talk about them when you
sit at home and when you walk along the road,
when you lie down and when you get up. Tie
them as symbols on your hands and bind them on
your foreheads. Write them on the doorframes of
your houses and on your gates.

Colossians 4:2—Devote yourselves to prayer, being
watchful and thankful.

**The Lord wants us to make him and his Word a regular part
of our family life also during the week. We do this through
regular Bible reading, family devotions, and prayers, as well
as through our Christian example.**

_._._._._._._._._._._._._._._._._

5. **WHO IS RESPONSIBLE FOR THE CHRISTIAN EDU-
CATION OF THE CHILDREN?**

2 Timothy 1:5—I have been reminded of your sincere
faith, which first lived in your grandmother Lois
and in your mother Eunice and, I am persuaded,
now lives in you also.

2 Timothy 3:15—From infancy you have known the
holy Scriptures, which are able to make you wise
for salvation through faith in Christ Jesus.

**It is the responsibility of Christian parents to pass on the
truths of their faith to their children.**

Ephesians 6:4—Fathers, do not exasperate your children; instead, bring them up in the training and
instruction of the Lord.

45

As the head of the family, the father is to take the lead in seeing to it that this is carried out.

> Ephesians 4:11,12—It was he who gave some to be apostles, some to be prophets, some to be evangelists, and some to be pastors and teachers, to prepare God's people for works of service, so that the body of Christ may be built up.
>
> John 21:15—"Feed my lambs."

The church is to assist the parents in carrying out this important task .

_ _ _ _ _ _ _ _ _ _ _ _ _ _ _ _ _ _ _ _

SUMMARY

Christ "married" us when we came to faith in him as our Savior. He entered into an eternal covenant with us that will be confirmed in heaven. He loved us so much that he lived and died in our place to earn eternal life for us. He did this even though we sinners did not deserve his love.

As Christ's bride we will show our love for him by worshiping him and serving him with our lives. We will give him first place in our lives by faithfully attending church, by holding family devotions, by praying to him, and by our Christian example.

While the church is there to assist, parents are primarily responsible for the Christian education of their children.

PRAYER TO END THE SESSION

Lord Jesus Christ, thank you for making us your bride. This is not something we deserved. Because of sin we were unfaithful to you and earned only your punishment. Yet you loved us so much that you cleansed us from our sin through your perfect life and sacrificial death on the cross.

46

We pray that in the future you would help us be a faithful bride. Make us eager to worship you and serve you with our lives, not only on weekends but throughout the week as well. Remind us that our relationship with you is like a beautiful home. It needs regular care and upkeep. Hear us for your sake. Amen.

FOR DISCUSSION:

1. A father is fulfilling his Christian responsibilities if he gets his family to church every Sunday and also makes sure his children attend Sunday school and confirmation class.

2. It is essential that a family spend time together even if it means missing church.

3. A faith that is not growing is dying.

4. Many families are too busy to hold family devotions.

5. Since infants and toddlers can be difficult to control, it is best to wait until they are older before taking them to church.

6. It is the responsibility of the church to give children a Christian education.

7. The best good works are those done for the church.

8. Washing dishes can be an act of worship to God.

9. Because of busy schedules most families no longer have time for midweek Lenten worship and other special services offered by the church.

10. The way a parent lives has a strong influence on a child.

PLEASE NOTE: Be sure to set a tentative day for *The Appraisal* found in Session 6. This should take place about a year after the wedding.

SESSION 6:

THE

APPRAISAL

(to be held about one year after the wedding)

Sometimes our house is appraised. This may happen when we buy or sell property. This appraisal may bring to light some improvements or repairs that need to be made. It's usually best to take care of these small items before they become major problems.

It works the same with marriage. You have been building your Christian home for about a year. Even though it may be a strong structure with a solid foundation, it's still good to give it an appraisal from time to time. That's the purpose of this session. With the help of the Marriage Appraisal presented on the following pages, you can evaluate your relationship. In this way you can build a Christian home that is even stronger.

MARRIAGE APPRAISAL

On a scale of 1 to 5 rate yourself in the following areas. Be sure that you are rating yourself and not your marriage partner. After doing so, discuss the list with your marriage partner together with your pastor. You are also free to discuss other matters that aren't covered by this appraisal.

	Weak →	Strong →
1. Listening to marriage partner	1 2 3 4 5	
2. Communicating with marriage partner	1 2 3 4 5	
3. Complimenting marriage partner	1 2 3 4 5	
4. Accepting role in marriage	1 2 3 4 5	
5. Admitting mistakes and seeking forgiveness	1 2 3 4 5	

	Weak Strong
6. Forgiving marriage partner	1 2 3 4 5
7. Working on romantic love	1 2 3 4 5
8. Managing time	1 2 3 4 5
9. Participating in activities that improve spiritual life (church attendance, Bible study, prayer life, etc.)	1 2 3 4 5
10. Managing finances	1 2 3 4 5
11. Leaving and cleaving (making the break from parents, etc.)	1 2 3 4 5
12. Cultivating Christian tone in home	1 2 3 4 5

List other items you would like to rate or discuss:

_____   1 2 3 4 5

_____   1 2 3 4 5

_____   1 2 3 4 5

BUILDING
THE CHRISTIAN HOME

PART 2

The Carpenter
Teaches
His Trade

THE CARPENTER TEACHES HIS TRADE

"Lord, teach us to pray."
Luke 11:1

Usually a triangular relationship is something to avoid. The saying "two's company, three's a crowd" has a lot of truth to it, especially when it comes to marriage. God ordained marriage to be the union of two people—not three or four or more. And yet, in one important sense, a Christian marriage does involve a triangular relationship: husband, wife, and Christ. Only with Christ as the third person can a marriage be Christian.

Making Christ the third person in your marriage is not a one-time event that takes place when you are married in his house. It's an ongoing process. Just as your relationship with each other needs to grow, so does your relationship with Christ.

One thing that's vital to a growing relationship is good communication. And communication is a two-way street. It involves both listening and speaking. Jesus recognized this with his disciples. He not only gave them his Word; at their request he also taught them to pray. He knew that to build a strong relationship with their Lord they would not only need to hear his Word. They would also need an active prayer life.

This section is designed to do the same for us. Each subject has a Scripture reading in which God speaks to us. That, in turn, is followed by a prayer in which we speak to God using some of the thoughts found in the reading. Just as Jesus taught his disciples effective communication, so through his Word the Carpenter of Nazareth continues to teach us his trade today. The result is that we will communicate more effectively with our heavenly Father and build a stronger relationship with Christ.

DAILY LIFE

LOW SELF-ESTEEM

Scripture Reading: 1 Peter 2:9

Lord, when we stand before you and look into the mirror of your perfect law, we have to admit we are worthless. We have sinned against you and cannot claim any value or worth for ourselves. Yet you still love us. Why? We don't know. You simply love us because you love us. And in your love you made us something special. You made us a chosen people, a royal priesthood, a holy nation, a people belonging to you. Lord, sometimes we get depressed and don't feel that we are worth much to anyone. But that's not true. We are worth a lot to you. And what greater sense of worth can we have than to know we are loved by you, the Creator of the universe, that you know us personally, that you have made us something special, that you gave up your own Son, Jesus Christ, to die for us. Thank you for placing such a high value on us even though we were worthless sinners. Thank you for loving us and saving us through Christ.

WORKAHOLISM

Scripture Reading: Ecclesiastes 1:2-11

Gracious Father, you warned us that life wouldn't be easy. You told us that by the sweat of our brow we would eat our food. You have instructed us that if anyone will not work neither should he eat. Yet there's more to life than work. There's you! Sometimes we get distracted by other things and slowly push you out of our lives. We get so wrapped up in our work schedule that we forget about you. We desperately try to fit you into our busy schedule yet all seems in vain. Please help us realize such a hectic pace is meaningless. Help us slow down and work our lives around you instead of trying to fit you into our lives. Help us take the time to enjoy the spiritual rest we have through Jesus' redemptive work. Bless us with productive labor. But also make us realize that unless we labor with you—and for you—we labor in vain.

FATIGUE AND TIME PRESSURE

Scripture Reading: 1 Kings 19:9-18

Father, it seems time is an endangered species. Appointments, meetings, activities, social gatherings—all of these can take up our time. They make our house resemble an airport more than a home. One person flies in, the other flies out. Neither pauses long enough to say hello. There seems to be no end to the various people and groups that compete for our time. The shouts of each one become louder and louder in an effort to get our attention. In a world like this your gospel is something we can really appreciate. It doesn't come in flashy colors. It isn't announced by drum rolls. It doesn't resort to gimmicks. It comes as a gentle whisper. Don't ever let the noise of life deaden our ears to that still small voice. Tune us in to that gentle whisper of the gospel, which shows us the peace and rest we have in Christ, even as we live in an otherwise restless world.

WORRY

Scripture Reading: Matthew 6:25-34

Heavenly Father, we realize we are to be faithful managers of all you give us, and so we are to be concerned about our lives. We are to be concerned about putting food on the table. We are to be concerned about our physical appearance. There is a fine line, though, between concern and worry. We want to be concerned about these things. Often we end up worrying about them. We worry about things over which we have little or no control. Please replace our worry with trust. For the more we trust you for everything, including the basic needs of life, the less we will worry about them. You gave your Son, Jesus Christ, to die for us. In doing so, you took care of our spiritual needs. You provided us with eternal life. Certainly you will take care of our physical needs as well.

MATERIALISM

Scripture Reading: 1 Timothy 6:9,10

Lord God, you have blessed us with so much. You have blessed us with a standard of living such as people in other parts of the world can only dream about. You have given us conveniences our parents or grandparents never imagined. We thank you for them. Lead us to a deeper appreciation of these many blessings. Most of all, make us content with what we have. As we look at friends and neighbors who have more than we have, we may become envious. We think if we only had a nicer home or a new car or that extra spending money, then we would be content. But happiness isn't found in material wealth. We are born with nothing. We die with nothing—at least we can't take with us what we have accumulated during our life. Those who make material gain their goal in life end up getting caught in a trap they can't escape. Lord, you have given us the greatest riches in the world. You have made us eternally rich in Christ. Through him we have the riches of forgiveness and eternal life. These are worth more than all the wealth of the world. Remind us that we are eternally rich. And make us content with whatever earthly blessings you choose to give us.

DEPRESSION

Scripture Reading: Psalm 42:11

O Lord, sometimes life just doesn't seem worth living. I look around at everything I have—friends, family, health, and wealth—yet nothing seems to cheer me up. I feel like throwing in the towel and calling it quits. Everything seems so hopeless. Help me put my hope in you. Help me see the value of life. Help me see the good my problems bring. Remind me that I'm not the only one to have problems. Many other people are going through the same trials and difficulties I am experiencing right now. Life is going to have its ups and downs. You have told us that. Even your Son, Jesus, faced overwhelming obstacles. He had to bear all the sins of the world. That wasn't an easy task, but he endured. And in doing so, he removed the greatest obstacle we face, the most depressing thing on earth. He removed the curse of sin, eternal death. Use this good news to lift me up emotionally and spiritually. While I am here in this life, fill me with a desire to praise you and declare your praises. Send your Holy Spirit to lift up my heart. And give me the zeal to worship and serve you, my Savior and my God, even when problems get me down.

LONELINESS

Scripture Reading: Matthew 26:56

Jesus Christ, you know what it's like to be alone. You were all alone in those last hours before your death. Those who had spent several years at your side, those who promised to stick with you through thick and thin, those who were determined to stay with you no matter what—those friends deserted you. When you needed them most, they were nowhere to be found. You had to stand before the Jewish leaders and before Pilate, you had to walk that long and lonely path to the cross, and you had to do it alone. While you were hanging on the cross, God himself turned his back on you and forsook you. Jesus, you know what it's like to be alone—completely alone. Sometimes we get pretty lonely. We feel we have no friends. We feel no one really cares about us. Yet you are our friend. And you care. You cared enough to die for us. Thanks for being our friend. Most of all, thanks for being our Savior.

PATIENCE

Scripture Reading: Romans 12:12

Lord in heaven, give me greater patience. Make me more patient with the children and with my marriage partner. Make me more patient with friends and relatives. Make me more patient with the people I see every day. And make me more patient with you. Patience isn't a popular thing. We live in an age where people want everything and they want it now. But now may not be the right time to have what I want. There may be some value in waiting for it. Make me patient with you. You know what's best for me. You are patient with me. Even though I continue to sin daily, you are patient and forgive me for Jesus' sake. Please give me such a patience in my everyday life. I patiently and faithfully pray in Jesus' name.

LOVE

Scripture Reading: 1 John 4:10,19

Gracious Lord, why is it that in a world that does so much talking about love, so little real love is found? And why do we who know what love is all about, who through Christ have experienced the greatest form of love that exists, why do we show so little of that love to others? Forgive us for our lack of love. Open our eyes to the love you have shown us. You have given us the perfect definition of love. "This is love: not that we loved you, but that you loved us and sent your Son as an atoning sacrifice for our sins." Without you we wouldn't know what true love is. We would be as confused as the unbelieving world is about love. Thank you for showing us what real love is. Thank you for teaching us how to love. With the apostle John we can truly say, "We love because you first loved us." In the name of our loving Savior we pray.

POSITIVE ATTITUDE

Scripture Reading: Philippians 4:8

Lord God in heaven, no one is born with a positive attitude. We are born with sinful hearts—hearts that are the source of negative comments, critical statements, pessimistic views, and loveless thoughts. When we came to faith, however, something changed in us. Our hearts were changed from hearts dead in sin to hearts alive in Christ. Unfortunately, our hearts will never be completely purged from all sin in this life. We won't experience that joy until we see you face to face in heaven. But, even though we are still sinful, we can strive to live by the Spirit. We can think by the Spirit. We can walk and talk by the Spirit. When we do this our attitude will change. For what can be more positive than the Christian faith? It has to do with such positive things as forgiveness, peace, joy, and life. Even your law with its prohibitions and condemnations has a positive goal in mind. Its crushing blows prepare us for the healing power of the gospel. We ask you to help us live as Christians who reflect the positive, loving, and joyful attitude of the gospel. It tells us the most positive message on earth: eternal life is ours through Christ.

MARRIED LIFE

COMMITMENT IN MARRIAGE

Scripture Reading: Matthew 19:4-6

Gracious Savior Jesus Christ, you showed us what it means to be committed to something. You were committed to us and to our eternal deliverance. You promised you would live a perfect life and die a sacrificial death in our place. And you kept that promise. There were many obstacles you faced on the way to the cross. There were many times when your patience was pushed to the limit. Yet you had made a promise, and you were determined to keep it. You were committed to that promise. As husband and wife we have also made a promise, a commitment, that we will remain faithful to each other for the rest of our lives. Like you we face many temptations to break this commitment. It often seems easier to walk away from a problem than to work through it. Remind us of the important promise we made on our wedding day, and the many blessings we will enjoy by keeping it. Keeping a promise as important as this won't be easy. But with your strength and guidance we know it can be done. Thank you for keeping your promise to us. You promised to die for us and you kept that promise. You have promised us eternal life, and we know you will keep that promise as well. Help us keep our promise and remain faithful to each other— and to you.

ROMANTIC LOVE

Scripture Reading: Genesis 24:67

Lord Jesus in heaven, Isaac had not even seen Rebekah before his marriage. He knew little or nothing about her. Yet he married her and loved her. To us this seems strange. In our society we marry out of love. We meet someone, fall in love, and decide to get married. Our parents played little part in arranging our marriage. They may have guided and encouraged us, but finally it was our choice and we chose to get married because we love each other. However, there is something we can learn from this marriage of Isaac and Rebekah. They didn't have a deep love for each other when they were married, for they hardly knew each other. Yet they were committed to each other as husband and wife, and from there the love grew. Lord, don't ever let us think that love is just something we fall in and out of. Our feelings will fluctuate from day to day. Love is more than a feeling—it's a commitment. We are reminded of the way you loved us. Your love is a committed love. It led you to die for us. Give us such a committed love. For when we base our marriage on our lifelong commitment of love and remain faithful to that commitment, from there the feelings of love will grow.

COMMUNICATION

Scripture Reading: Ephesians 4:29

Heavenly Father, communication is what makes the world go around. So much time is wasted, so many mistakes are made, so many things are not done—all because of a breakdown in communication. In a relationship as close as a marriage, good communication is essential. Why, then, is it that we so often fail to communicate effectively with the one we love? We are reluctant to share inner feelings; we lash out with biting remarks; we avoid subjects that need to be discussed. All of this destroys a relationship. Good communication isn't easy. No one does it perfectly. But don't let us use that as an excuse for not trying. In your Word you communicated the most important message there is. You told us that, though we are sinners, we have a Savior in Christ. We realize the need for communication in our marriage. Give us the knowledge and skill to fulfill that need with effective, meaningful communication.

FORGIVENESS

Scripture Reading: Colossians 3:12-14

Gracious Lord, no marriage is perfect, for marriage involves two sinful human beings. That's why you are so specific about telling husbands and wives to love each other—and to forgive each other. If anyone has a right to tell us to be more forgiving, it's you. You are perfect, sinless, and righteous. We are imperfect, sinful, and unrighteous. Yet you love us and forgive us for Jesus' sake. Forgiving sounds like such an easy thing to do. But in real life it's not. It means forgiving someone who has hurt us deeply. When we are reluctant to forgive or seek forgiveness, direct us to the cross. There you forgave the sins of the world—freely and completely. That is how we are to forgive. We are to forgive as the Lord forgave us.

COMPANIONSHIP

Scripture Reading: Genesis 2:18-24

Lord, shortly after you created the first man you commented that something wasn't good. You saw a void in his life. He was alone, and that wasn't good. Man had the companionship of the animals. He also enjoyed a close and personal relationship with you. Yet you noted that he was alone. He lacked human companionship, and so you made a helper suitable to him. You created a companion. You made woman. In bringing the first woman to the first man you instituted marriage. We thank you for the blessed companionship we enjoy in marriage. Often we take it for granted. We don't realize how much we enjoy the company of our marriage partner until we are apart for a while. It isn't good for us to be alone. Thank you for giving us marriage and blessing us with this kind of companionship. As we enjoy the companionship of each other, draw us closer to Christ and the blessed companionship we have through faith in him as our Savior.

SEXUAL HAPPINESS

Scripture Reading: Matthew 19:5

Father, no human relationship is more meaningful and intimate than the sexual union. Our sinful heart is quick to abuse and degrade this beautiful gift and reduce it to nothing more than a self-gratifying act. Our sinful heart makes us think that real sexual happiness is found outside of marriage. But that's not the case. People who live an immoral life may give the impression they are happy. They may even find temporary pleasure. But they haven't found real sexual happiness. This can be found only in marriage. Keep us faithful to each other. And help us love each other physically, not in a self-seeking way, but in a self-giving way, even as Jesus gave himself for us in unselfish love.

ANGER

Scripture Reading: Ephesians 4:26

Lord in heaven, even in a strong marriage there are going to be conflicts. As imperfect partners we do things that annoy and hurt each other. This can lead to anger. Lord, make us realize a strong marriage is not one in which the partners never feel angry. It's one where the partners use conflicts constructively—to build rather than destroy. When we feel angry, help us control it so we do not sin in our anger. Conflict can be a beneficial thing, but only when it's dealt with in a patient and loving manner, and only when disagreements are resolved on a regular basis. Because we are sinners, you have every right to be eternally angry with us. But you are not. Instead you took out your anger on Christ and punished him in our place. Lead us to appreciate what you did through your Son, so that we will never sin in our anger.

HUSBANDS

Scripture Reading: Ephesians 5:25-33

"Husbands, love your wives." Lord, these words seem so self-evident. Of course husbands love their wives. Isn't that why a man marries a woman? Isn't it because he loves her? Why, then, are you so explicit in telling husbands to love their wives? Well, the fact is that there are as many different kinds of love as there are colors in the rainbow. When you tell husbands to love their wives, you have a special type of love in mind. You say, "Husbands, love your wives as Christ loved the church." We thank you for calling us to faith in your Son as our Savior. Through faith we know what great love you have for us, your church. It's no wonder some husbands don't know how to love their wives. They don't know the deep love you showed your church. We know that love. We have seen it in Christ. We have experienced it through the many spiritual blessings we enjoy as your bride. Our efforts at imitating this love will fall far short. But with your help we can strive toward that goal of a perfect Christ-like love.

WIVES

Scripture Reading: Ephesians 5:22-24

Heavenly Father, words like "submit" and "obey" can sound so harsh and cruel. We immediately think of a slave submitting to his master and jumping to his every wish. Yet this is not what you have in mind when you tell wives to submit to their husbands. This submission is to resemble the way the church submits to Christ. Slavish compulsion is not a part of our submission to you. You don't force us to do anything. You have set us free through the gospel and now give us the freedom to love you. That is also how we as wives are to love and submit to our husbands. We are to do so, not because we have to, but because we want to. Just as we trust that you are looking out for our best interests, so we trust our husbands. Just as we have given ourselves completely to you, so we give ourselves to our husbands in a totally committed submission. It isn't easy to give ourselves so completely to one person. It wasn't easy for Christ to give up his life for us either. Because of what you did for us, we find it easy to submit to you. The love of Christ compels us. May we have the same attitude toward our husbands.

LEAVING AND CLEAVING

Scripture Reading: Genesis 2:24

Lord God, many changes take place when a man and woman become husband and wife. Both leave their former families. No longer do they obey and serve their parents as children. Now they honor and respect them as adults. No longer are the old family ties of primary importance. Now a new family is formed. Please help us carry out this leaving and cleaving process gracefully. We will honor and love and care for our parents as long as they live. However, we are not to let our relationship with them interfere in our marriage. We are now a new family. We are now united to each other. This is why we left father and mother—to be united to each other. We did so to become one under Christ, and three with Christ.

THE BLESSING OF CHILDREN

FAMILY PLANNING

Scripture Reading: James 4:13-15

Almighty God, it is said, "Man proposes, God disposes." We can make plans, but you always have the final say. This is especially true when it comes to family planning. We can plan to have children. We can plan when we want to have them. And this is fine. You don't want us to enter marriage blindly. Nor do you want us to have a family without giving prior thought to the responsibility of raising children. However, as we sit back and evaluate all the time and money and energy that are spent raising children, we might conclude we could never afford even one child, much less two or three or more. Strengthen our trust in your Son as our Savior. And lead us to trust you also in this matter of family planning. You have told us you will help us. You will guide us. You will provide for our needs. Lord, we trust you. Lord, we believe you. Help us overcome our unbelief.

WISHING AND HOPING

Scripture Reading: 1 Samuel 1:1-20

Creator of life, our unbelieving society often feels that we human beings control everything in life. As your children we know this is not true. You guide us in life. You give us the gift of life. Open our eyes to the wisdom of your ways. Open our hearts to receive the blessing of a child when and if you choose to give it. Lord, if it be your will, bless us with a child. Entrust to us a new life to nurture and love. What you give to us, we will in turn give back to you. Through Holy Baptism the child will become your child and through your Word will remain your child. Please, Lord, bless us with this gift for the sake of your Son.

NEW ADDITION

Scripture Reading: Psalm 139:13-18

O Lord, we praise you for the beautiful way you bring a child into this world. What some call only a process of nature we know to be your special creative act. With the psalm writer we have to exclaim, "I praise you for I am fearfully and wonderfully made." We thank you for the new life you have placed into our care. We also thank you for the sacrament of Holy Baptism, by which our child will be given rebirth through water and the Spirit and be born into your family of believers. Give us the ability and wisdom to raise our child as your child, so that together with all believers, our child may enjoy the hope of heaven you give through Christ.

HOLY BAPTISM

Scripture Reading: Mark 10:13-19

Gracious Lord, we thank and praise you for the new life you have given us. We also thank you for the sacrament of Holy Baptism. In this special way, you make our child your child. Because we are sinful parents, we realize that as innocent as our child looks, this baby is sinful and deserves eternal punishment together with us all. But in Holy Baptism you give us a comforting promise. You promise that through the water and the Word our child will have a rebirth through the Spirit. The sins of this child will all be washed away. Our little one will become your child, a member of your family, and an heir of eternal life. During the years of growing and maturing, remind our child of the power of baptism. And help our child live this baptism daily. Make us faithful parents who water the seed of faith with the Word so that it may grow and mature and produce a generous harvest of the fruits of faith. Once again, thank you for Baptism.

DISCIPLINE

Scripture Reading: Proverbs 13:24

Lord in heaven, in your Word you say, "No discipline seems pleasant at the time, but painful." We remember the discipline our parents gave us. It brought tears to our eyes and pain to our hearts. At the time, we may have thought our parents were being mean and cruel. "If they really love me, why do they do this to me?" we wondered. But now we can see it was for our good. Our sinful nature was getting the best of us. Their discipline helped bring it back under control. As parents, we now realize the greatest pain isn't felt by the child but by the parent. It hurts when we have to discipline our children. Yet we know it's for their good. It is a way we show them love. "He who loves him is careful to discipline him," you have written. This is the same reason why you discipline us—because you love us and want us to be with you in heaven. You don't want anything to deprive us of the eternal life your Son earned by his suffering and death. Give us the strength to discipline our children lovingly and faithfully, just as you do with us. We want them to be with us in heaven.

SPIRITUAL TRAINING

Scripture Reading: Deuteronomy 6:5-9

Heavenly Father, you have commanded us: "Bring up your children in the training and instruction of the Lord." We recognize this as both a serious responsibility and a gracious privilege. It is an honor to share your Word with our children. We may be tempted to shift the responsibility to others. We may feel it is the job of the church or Christian school to carry it out. Both are gifts of God that assist us in this awesome task. Yet they are not there to replace us. Christian education is, first of all, the responsibility of parents. Both by Word and example we are to instruct our children in the Christian faith.

Help us take this job seriously. And help us carry it out effectively, for Jesus' sake.

SIBLING RIVALRY

Scripture Reading: Genesis 27:1—28:5

Gracious Lord, why do our children lash out at one another? Why do they make a game out of hurting one another? Why don't they show more love for one another? O Lord, we know the root of the problem is sin. Because our children are sinful human beings, they display hatred, selfishness, anger, and jealously. Even though they are brothers and sisters, they are not always filled with brotherly love. This doesn't mean we should accept the situation and do nothing to change it. It just means we have our work cut out for us. For just as the problem is sin, so the solution is Christ. Through the power of the Holy Spirit he can fill their sinful hearts with love. He can bring about a change in their lives. Yet this change will not take place overnight. It will be a lifelong process. Give us patience as well as firmness in dealing with our children. Help us endure the daily struggles and battles, remembering that raising the future generation isn't one quick and easy step. It's a long and difficult process that can last a lifetime. Without your help we would fail. With it we shall succeed.

STIR CRAZY

Scripture Reading: Luke 5:16

Lord Jesus, I'm at the end of my rope. The kids are screaming; the dog is barking; dinner was a disaster; the phone won't stop ringing; and the house is a mess. I feel I'm about to go crazy. You know what it's like. You had a busy ministry. People kept following you. They wouldn't leave you alone. There were those who were sick or hurting or confused. You saw how much they needed your time and attention. You wanted to help them, and you did. But there were also times when you needed to get away for awhile and rest. Please give me the physical rest I need. But most of all, show me the spiritual rest you give in the gospel. Help me set aside time for prayer and meditation on your Word. That's how you found the strength to face the pressures of your busy work. Such an approach will also do wonders for me.

ADOLESCENCE

Scripture Reading: Ecclesiastes 12:1-7

Father, our children are now entering a very critical time of life. They are at a crossroads. One road leads to you, the other to destruction. The forces that pull them down the road to destruction are great, and at times the children seem eager to follow that path. We want to reach out and pull them back, but that's not always the best thing to do. They are growing up and need more freedom. It's not time to set them completely free. They are not yet adults and are not ready for the responsibilities of adult life. But they are learning and growing—often by their mistakes—just as we did. As this process begins, give us the love to set them free gradually and gracefully. Send your Holy Spirit to strengthen their faith in Christ. Only then will they be able to resist the many pressures to conform to the unbelieving world. Please help them remember you, their Creator and Savior, during the days of their youth, as well as to their dying day—before the silver cord is severed, and the golden bowl is broken, and all is lost.

CHOOSING A PARTNER

Scripture Reading: Proverbs 31:30

Lord God, watch over our children as they begin to date. Even though it's been quite a few years since we were dating, we can remember those days quite well. As we look back we laugh at how awkward we felt at first. As time went on, the relationship grew and matured till finally we were standing before your altar, promising our love and faithfulness to each other. As our children begin dating, keep them pure in body and soul. You have given us the beautiful gift of sexual happiness. You have also told us to save it for marriage. As our children go about choosing partners for life, direct them to Christian marriage partners who share the belief we have in Jesus Christ and him crucified. Beauty and charm may keep things going for a while, but soon they fade. But a marriage built on you and your Son will be a marriage that lives—and lasts.

SPIRITUAL LIFE

OUR CALLING AS CHRISTIANS

Scripture Reading: Deuteronomy 7:6-11

Gracious Lord, there is no reason under the sun why you chose us to be your children. Like the people of Israel, we have grumbled and complained. At times we have rebelled against your laws. However, you still chose us to be your people, your treasured possession. It wasn't because we were better than other people, for we were not. It wasn't because we deserved to be chosen, for we did not. There is only one reason why you chose us to be Christians—your gracious love. As Moses told the Israelites, "It was because the LORD loved you." It wasn't because of a quality in us that you loved us. It was because of a quality in you—your love. We are not the reason for your love; you are. What a gracious privilege to be chosen as your people. Lead us to appreciate and honor our calling as Christians, and give us a greater trust in our Redeemer, Christ. By your grace and love, we are your chosen people, your treasured possession.

LETTING OUR LIGHT SHINE

Scripture Reading: Philippians 2:14-16; Ephesians 4:1

Lord God, when you called us to be Christians you also called us to live like Christians. The unbelieving world we live in fits perfectly the description Paul gives in Philippians: a crooked and depraved generation. Since we live in the world, we are influenced by its thinking and affected by its lifestyle. Sometimes the sad truth is that we live more like your enemies than your children. Lord, you have called us to be Christians. You have called us by the gospel and enlightened us by the Holy Spirit. You have called us to let that light of the gospel shine in our lives. Thank you for the privilege of being your shining stars. May we also recognize our responsibility to let our light shine and share your Word with others.

DEDICATION TO GOD

Scripture Reading: Romans 12:1-8

Heavenly Father, it sounds so easy to be a Christian. We become Christians by believing in Christ as our Savior. And you give us eternal life—freely and completely. "Believe on the Lord Jesus, and you will be saved," you tell us. Our efforts don't add a thing. But even though you don't want anything as far as our eternal life is concerned, you do want everything as far as our love and life are concerned. You ask us to deny ourselves. You tell us to offer ourselves as living sacrifices to you. This isn't an easy thing to do. It goes against our sinful nature. Our sinful self doesn't want to give you anything. Ironically, our old self also refuses to receive any gifts, especially the gift of eternal life. Heaven, however, isn't something we can earn on our own. We need your help and you give it to us through Christ. Of course, free grace is not cheap grace. It cost Christ his life. Recognizing this, how can we give anything less for you?

FAITHFUL TO THE WORD

Scripture Reading: Psalm 119:105-112

Lord in heaven, we need your help in being more faithful students of your Word. When we get too busy for Bible reading, slow us down. When we get lazy, get us going again. When we forget, remind us of what we are missing. You have given us your Word for two important reasons: to show us the way to eternal life and to guide us in our earthly life. When it comes to our earthly life, we easily lose our way and become lost. This is because we haven't used the lamp and light of your Word. In our baptism you made a covenant of grace with us, receiving us as your children, cleansing us of all sin, and guaranteeing that you will never leave us or forsake us. At our confirmation we promised that with your help we would remain faithful to you and suffer all, even death, rather than fall away from you. How can we even begin to keep this promise if we don't continue to read and study your Word? Fill our hearts with the sincere desire to keep your decrees and to read your Word as long as we live. Your Word centers on Christ and reading it is the way to keep our lives centered on him.

GOD'S HOUSE

Scripture Reading: Hebrews 10:25

Almighty God, it hardly seems necessary to remind us to go to church. For what could be more basic to Christianity—to religion in general—than public worship. An evaluation of our own attendance and attentiveness in your house would show we need this reminder. For we do not always share the enthusiasm of the psalm writer who declared, "I rejoiced with those who said to me, 'Let us go to the house of the LORD.'" The blessings we receive through public worship are countless. Our faith in Christ is strengthened through the Word. We receive encouragement from the Word and from one another. And we give encouragement to others simply by being in church. Instead of making a habit of skipping church, help us get into the habit of gathering together with our fellow Christians regularly. For we know the Day is approaching fast.

BACKSLIDING

Scripture Reading: Revelation 3:14-22

Lord, we have to admit we haven't exactly been giving you first place in our lives. Our faith has been put on the back burner. We have become apathetic in our faith. We got so busy with our jobs, our lives, ourselves, that we forgot about you. Yet forgetting about you isn't easy to do. How often didn't we feel guilty about our neglect of you and your Word and with good reason. We are guilty! It is a sin to place anything on a higher priority than you. It is a sin to neglect you. It is a sin to be apathetic in the faith. And we are guilty of these sins. We come to you asking your forgiveness for Jesus' sake. Remove the lukewarm water of apathy from our hearts. Send your Holy Spirit to rekindle the fires of faith. We don't know when you will take us out of this world. You take young and old alike, those who are ready and those who are not. We want to be ready when you come. That's why we want to keep our spiritual house in order at all times.

THE LORD'S SUPPER

Scripture Reading: Luke 22:19,20

Lord Jesus, in many ways our relationship with you resembles a marriage. At our baptism you "married" us. You pledged us your love and faithfulness. You told us you loved us and that we were your bride. This is similar to the promise a man and woman make to each other on their wedding day. Yet a husband doesn't just tell his wife he loves her on that day. Every day he continues to assure his wife, "I love you. I am committed to you. I am your husband and will remain faithful to you." You also give us this regular assurance through your Word. Daily you tell us, "I still love you. I forgive you. I am committed to you as my bride." And the Lord's Supper is a special way you assure us of your love. We could compare this to a birthday or wedding anniversary. At times like that, a husband may show his love in a special way. He doesn't just tell his wife he loves her. He gives her a card or gift or flowers. This is what you do in the Lord's Supper. You give us a special, personal assurance of the forgiveness you earned on the cross. You give us your own body and blood as a pledge of your love. Don't ever let us forget what a special blessing you give us in this sacrament of the altar. Instead, make us more faithful in receiving it. It's a special way of showing that we are yours and you are ours forever.

DAILY WORSHIP

Scripture Reading: 1 Corinthians 10:31

Lord, we divide our day into various parts. Part of the day we spend eating, part of the day working, part of the day relaxing, part of the day sleeping. Because each activity gets only a part of our day, a part of our lives, we might be tempted to devote to you only a part of our life. We take time for you on Sunday morning or at the end of a busy day when we say our prayers. That is the part of the day we spend worshiping you. While you do want us to set aside specific time for worship and prayer, you also ask that we devote our whole life to you, whether we are eating, relaxing, or working. Your Word has told us that whatever we do, we are to do it all for the glory of God. Our life is to be a worship service to you. Christ devoted his whole life to save us sinners. May we spend our whole life praising and thanking him for that.

CHURCH FAMILY

Scripture Reading: Romans 15:4-6

Lord of the church, we have a lot in common with our fellow Christians at church. We may not share common interests in areas such as hobbies or recreation. We may have personalities that are quite different. In spite of this, we do have our most precious possession in common. We share a special bond as Christians. Through faith we are united with Christ. And we are united with one another through Christ. This is a bond which can support us in our troubles, strengthen us in our faith, and make our lives happier. Lord, we thank you for this special unity we enjoy as a church family and the many blessings it gives. May we always appreciate this bond we share with you through faith. May we never hesitate to express it and share it with our family at home as well as with our larger family at church. And may we always have the courage and zeal to invite others into this blessed union with you and into this happy family of ours at church.

OUR MARRIAGE WITH CHRIST

Scripture Reading: Hosea 2:16,19,20

Lord Jesus Christ, we have been unfaithful to you not once but many times. We didn't deserve to be your slave, much less your bride. Yet in your grace and love you took us as your bride. Why you did this we don't know. It is a mystery we will never understand this side of eternity. You made us your bride. You entered into the closest possible relationship with us! We can't even begin to express our thanks and gratitude. When we feel alone, when we are unsure and become filled with doubts, remind us who we are. We are members of your church. We are your spiritual bride, the bride you cleansed from sin by the washing with water through the Word, the bride you presented to God as a radiant church, without stain or wrinkle or any other blemish, the bride you loved so much you gave up your life to save her. It is a great honor to be your bride. May our marriage with you be a source of comfort and strength also in our earthly marriage to each other.

THE FINAL FRONTIER

GROW OLD WITH ME

Scripture Reading: Isaiah 46:4

Lord God, because of sin, growing old is a reality of life. It is difficult in many ways. It's painful to watch ourselves grow old. We may be wiser but we are also weaker. And it's frustrating when we can't do things we once did. It hurts when one friend after another is taken away from us. All of this is a constant reminder—we are growing old. Yet, as you have been with us in every other stage of life, so you are with us now. You don't desert us at a certain age. Because you have made us and redeemed us through your Son, we know you will sustain us and carry us even in old age. We could never have made it this far without you. And now that we are entering the final frontier of our lives, we trust you will continue to be with us. Help us explore the beauties of this vast new wilderness before us and keep us safe on the narrow road that leads to our heavenly home.

THE BEST IS YET TO BE

Scripture Reading: Romans 8:18-39

Heavenly Father, when we were young we used to hope and dream about better times to come. We would think about settling down in our dream house. We would look ahead to that time when we wouldn't have to worry so much about working and making money. We would dream about retirement, when we would finally do some traveling and get to all those other things we never had time for when we were working. Now that the time is here, how often don't we think back and reminisce about the "good old days." Because of poor health or tired bodies, we wish we were young again. Father, remind us that we are not drawing to the end of our lives. The best part of our life is not over. The best is yet to be. How beautifully you bring this out in these words from Romans. As you point out to us, nothing in all the world can compare to the glory that will be revealed in us. Nothing in all creation can separate us from the love of God that is in Christ Jesus, our Lord. Thank you for comforting us with this truth that the best is yet to be. We are confident the best that is yet to be will be a reality because of our Savior's atoning death and victorious resurrection.

EMPTY NEST

Scripture Reading: Ecclesiastes 3:1-8

Almighty God, when we were young we enjoyed the springtime of life. Everything was fresh and new, and we anticipated getting out of school and starting a career. Then there was the excitement of dating and finding a mate for life. Together we built our nest and as time went on you filled it with young. We spent the summer of life raising our children. We watched them grow and spread their wings. Now summer is over and the nest is empty. The children have flown off to lives of their own. This has left us feeling we no longer serve a purpose in life. In the past we felt needed; now it seems our lives are meaningless. That would be true if you hadn't sent your Son to be our Savior. But you did! And in Christ you give eternal life to our souls and meaning to our lives. Because of what Christ did, every season of life has meaning, including the autumn of life we are in right now. And even though winter is ahead, we know that season will also bring a beauty all its own. For Solomon has told us, "There is a time for everything, and a season for every activity under heaven."

LONELINESS

Scripture Reading: Psalm 71

Gracious Lord Jesus Christ, you have promised to be with us to the very end of the age. And that also includes old age.

We don't get to see our children as often as we would like. Many of our friends have gone their separate ways—some to their eternal homes, others to different places or in pursuit of other interests. This gives us a feeling of loneliness. Yet as much as we miss our children and friends, we know we are not alone. We have the companionship of each other. You instituted marriage and blessed it with companionship. And as you have assured us through the psalm writer, we have the companionship of you. You watch over us. You protect us. You comfort us. You are a friend who is there at all times. And you are never too busy to listen. Because of this, we are never alone, not even in old age. As our friend, you are always there. And there's another thing you don't want us to forget: you are not only our friend, you are also our Savior and God.

HEALTH

Scripture Reading: Psalm 103:1-5

Father, some people say, "As long as you have your health, you have everything." Good health is a blessing we pray for and appreciate. But we also realize you may take away our health, and for a good reason. We can't always see your purpose at the time. You don't always tip your hand so we can see how you are playing the cards. But one thing we are sure of— the suffering you send us is for our good. It helps us remember we are mortal sinners. It draws us closer to you, who forgives all sins in Christ and heals all our diseases according to your will. It gives us a deep appreciation for what heaven will be like, where we will be free from all disease and death. Thank you for the good health you have given us. Give us the strength to endure sickness and other suffering. And may the hymn of praise always be on our lips, "Praise the LORD, O my soul; all my inmost being praise his holy name. Praise the LORD, O my soul, and forget not all his benefits."

FOR OUR CHILDREN

Scripture Reading: 2 Timothy 1:3-7

Giver of all life, you have blessed us with children. We raised them, fed them, guided them, and loved them. We also had the privilege of teaching them the Christian faith. Timothy had a mother and a grandmother who saw the need to instruct him in your Word. They fulfilled this need to the best of their ability. We confess we have not been perfect parents. We did anything but a perfect job in teaching our children your Word. Yet we tried our best to share with them the truth you shared with us. When it comes to obeying your command to go and make disciples of all nations, our families are our first priority. Evangelism begins at home. Please cause the seed of the Word we have planted in our children to grow. We want our children to always know your Son as their Savior. We want them to be saved. We want them to be with us and you in heaven.

GRANDCHILDREN

Scripture Reading: Psalm 128

Lord in heaven, thank you for the children you have given us. Thank you for the children you have given our children. It is a joy to see and hold and love our children's children. As we prayed for our children, so we pray for our grandchildren. Protect them from all spiritual and physical harm. Give them a strong trust in your Son, Jesus Christ, as their Savior. Help them withstand the many temptations they will face as the end draws near. Instill in them a deep desire to fear you and walk in your ways, so that before your throne in heaven we may rejoice with our children, their children, and the believers of all generations to come. Together we will worship you as the God and Savior of all.

THE VALUE OF LIFE

Scripture Reading: Psalm 92:12-15

Almighty Father, we live in a society that places a great deal of value on youth. And so we dye our hair. We apply cosmetics. We try to hide the wrinkles on our face. We spend much time and money covering the signs of age. We know it's not wrong to do this. You want us to take care of our personal appearance. But as we do, remind us that human worth doesn't depend on such temporary things as beauty and youth. This is how the unbelieving world determines worth. But this is not your way. Every human being is valuable to you. You are not willing that any should perish. You gave your Son to die for all people—young and old alike. And until you call us home we have a purpose in this life. We are here to praise and worship you. We are here to tell others about you, to proclaim your name to the ends of the earth. Lord, we may have retired from our job, but don't ever let us feel that we are also retired from a useful and productive life. Use us for your purpose. Use us to bear fruit for you, even in old age.

DEATH

Scripture Reading: Psalm 23

Lord Jesus, why is it so hard to die? We all know it's going to happen. And we have a lifetime to prepare for it. Why, then, is it so hard to die? The reason is that death isn't natural. It's unnatural. You created people to live, not to die. Yet sin changed all that. Sin brought death into the world. Even though thoughts about death may strike fear into our hearts, we don't have to grieve like those who have no hope. You died and rose again. You have given us a living hope in the resurrection of Christ. You have destroyed death and have brought life and immortality to light through the gospel. You have given us the promise, "Because I live, you also will live." In order to get to our heavenly home we have to walk through the valley of the shadow of death. That is painful. But we know we will not stay in the valley. As our Good Shepherd you will lead us through that valley of death. You will lead us to the green pastures and the quiet waters of our heavenly home.

WHEN DEATH PARTS US

Scripture Reading: 2 Timothy 4:6-8

Eternal God, you have taken from me something that can never be replaced. You have taken away a part of me. As I think back I can recall many happy memories. There were those times when we were dating and just getting to know each other, that day when we agreed we wanted to get married. I can still recall the day as though it was yesterday. Then there were those days of preparation leading up to the big event—our wedding day. We worried and wondered if everything would work out, and it did. You were there, and you helped us through. We pledged our love and faithfulness to each other for life. But that was only the beginning. As the years went by, you helped us build on that foundation. You blessed us with children. Together we watched them grow. Together we raised them as best we could. Together we watched each of them begin a new life and form a new family. We faced many hardships but you were there, and you helped us through. Then we entered that final frontier of life. We grew old together. We realized what a blessed companionship we shared for those many years and still did share. Now, Lord, it is over. We promised to remain faithful till death parted us. Now we have been parted by death. You have taken away from me a friend—the closest friend I had in this life. As much as it tears me apart, I am confident I will see my friend again. You have assured us of that happy reunion all believers will have with you in heaven. Comfort me with this knowledge.

91

Until the time comes for me to pass from this final frontier to the new frontier of eternal life, make me see my purpose for being here. Help me fight the good fight of faith. Help me finish the race. Help me keep the faith. Then I, too, will receive the crown of righteousness which you will give to me, not because I was such a good marriage partner, not because I was such a good parent, not because of anything I did, but solely because your Son, Jesus Christ, died for my sins and rose as proof of my resurrection.

BUILDING
THE CHRISTIAN HOME

PART 3

**More
Building
Blocks**

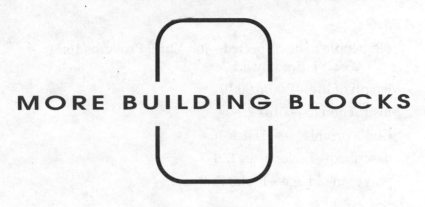

MORE BUILDING BLOCKS

A Biblical Index for the Family

ABORTION

life begins at conception—Psalm 139:13-18; Jeremiah 1:5

God forbids taking of life—Exodus 20:13; 1 John 3:15

Old Testament penalty for killing unborn—
    Exodus 21:22-25

ADOLESCENCE

listen to parents—Proverbs 13:1; 23:22

remember God in youth—Ecclesiastes 11:7—12:8;
    1 Timothy 4:12; 2 Timothy 2:22

ADULTERY

breaks marriage bond—Matthew 19:9

begins in heart—Matthew 5:28; 15:19

condemned—1 Corinthians 6:9,10,15,16; Galatians 5:19-21

warnings against—Proverbs 2:12-19; 5:1-23; 6:20-29; 7:1-27

purity commanded—1 Corinthians 6:18-20; Romans 13:13;
    1 Timothy 5:22

not the unforgivable sin—John 8:10,11; Luke 7:36-50

AGING

old people to be respected—Job 12:12; Proverbs 16:31; 23:22; 1 Timothy 5:1,2

length of life—Psalm 90:10

instruction to—Titus 2:2

God's promise to—Isaiah 46:4

described—Ecclesiastes 12:1-7

prayer in old age—Psalm 71:9

ALCOHOL

warnings against drunkenness—Proverbs 23:20,21,29-35; Luke 21:34; Ephesians 5:18; 1 Corinthians 6:9,10

do not give or take offense—Romans 14:1—15:2

moderation—Psalm 104:14,15; 1 Timothy 5:23

ANGER

negative results of—Proverbs 14:17,29; 15:18; 22:24,25

warned against—Psalm 37:8; Ecclesiastes 7:9; Matthew 5:22; Galatians 5:19-21; Ephesians 4:26,27,31; Colossians 3:8; 1 Timothy 2:8; James 1:19-20

God's holy anger over sin—Exodus 34:6,7; Psalm 2:12

BAPTISM

commanded by Christ—Matthew 28:19

offers eternal life—Mark 16:16; Titus 3:5-7; 1 Peter 3:20,21

offers forgiveness of sins—Acts 2:38,39; 22:16

for all people (including children)—Matthew 28:19; Acts 2:39

gives power to live Christian life—Romans 6:4; Galatians 3:27

only one—Ephesians 4:5

infants can believe—Matthew 18:6

infants are born sinful—Genesis 8:21; Psalm 51:5; John 3:6

BIRTH CONTROL

procreation a blessing of marriage—Genesis 1:28

husband should show concern for wife—1 Peter 3:7

children are a blessing from God—Genesis 33:5;
Psalm 127:3

warnings against materialism—Psalm 10:2,3;
Proverbs 23:4,5; Luke 12:15; 1 Timothy 6:6-10

CHILDREN (see also DISCIPLINE)

a blessing—Genesis 33:5; Psalm 127:3; Proverbs 17:6

spiritual training of—Deuteronomy 6:6-9; Ephesians 6:4

COMMUNICATION

speak the truth—Ephesians 4:15,25-27; Colossians 3:9;
Psalm 34:11-14

forgiving attitude—Colossians 3:12-14

speak to build up—Proverbs 16:24; Ephesians 4:29

dangers of gossip—Proverbs 11:13; 16:28; 19:5

warnings—Matthew 12:36; 1 Timothy 5:13; James 3:6

compliment marriage partner—Song of Songs 1:15,16;
4:1-7; 5:10-16

defend others—Proverbs 31:8,9

CONFIDENCE (see SELF-ESTEEM)

DATING

qualities of good wife—Proverbs 31:10-31; 1 Peter 3:3,4

warning against sexual immorality—1 Timothy 5:22

DISCIPLINE

God's discipline of us—Proverbs 6:23; Hebrews 12:11

of children—Proverbs 19:18; 22:6,15; 23:13,14; Ephesians 6:4; Colossians 3:21

lack of—1 Samuel 2:12-25; 2 Kings 2:23-25

DIVORCE

God's anger at—Malachi 2:14-16

problem begins in heart—Matthew 5:27,28

for marital unfaithfulness—Matthew 19:3-12

for desertion—1 Corinthians 7:10-17

forgiveness for—Luke 7:36-50; John 8:10,11

ENDURANCE

in trials—Romans 8:18-39; James 1:2-4,12

prayer for—Romans 15:4-6; 1 Thessalonians 1:3

in doing good—Galatians 6:9

FORGIVENESS

of enemies—Proverbs 25:21,22

of others—Matthew 6:14,15; 18:15-35; Ephesians 4:32; Colossians 3:13

of sexual sins—John 8:1-11; Luke 7:36-50

of sins of youth—Psalm 25:7

from God—Exodus 34:6; Psalm 19:12; 103:8-13; Luke 15:11-31; 1 John 2:1,2

HOMOSEXUALITY

condemned—Romans 1:24-27; 1 Corinthians 6:9,10

HUMILITY

imitate Christ—Philippians 2:3-11

imitate little children—Matthew 18:2-4

praised—Proverbs 15:33; 16:19; 22:4; Matthew 5:3; 20:26,27; Romans 12:3; 1 Corinthians 10:12

HUSBAND

responsibilities of—Ephesians 5:25-33; Colossians 3:19; 1 Timothy 5:8; 1 Peter 3:7

INFIDELITY (see ADULTERY)

IN-LAW RELATIONSHIP

leave and cleave—Genesis 2:24

JEALOUSY

dangers of—Proverbs 27:4; Ecclesiastes 4:4

in marriage—Proverbs 6:34; Romans 13:13; 1 Corinthians 3:3

in Old Testament marriage—Numbers 5:11-31

JOY

in the Lord—Nehemiah 8:10; Psalm 100:1-3; Philippians 4:4-7; 1 Thessalonians 5:16

over salvation—Luke 10:20; 1 Peter 1:8

fruit of the Spirit—Romans 14:17; 15:13; Galatians 5:22

in trials—Romans 12:12; James 1:2; 1 Peter 4:13

LOVE (see also ROMANTIC LOVE)

described—1 Corinthians 13:1-13; 1 John 4:10

in marriage—Ephesians 5:22-33

for others—John 15:13; Romans 13:8-10; Colossians 3:12-14

greatness of God's love—Ephesians 3:17-19; 1 John 4:9

MAN (see WOMAN—Role of Man and Woman)

MARRIAGE

lifelong—Matthew 19:9; Romans 7:1,2; 1 Corinthians 7:39

union—Genesis 2:24; Matthew 19:8,9

to be honored—Proverbs 18:22; 1 Timothy 5:14; Hebrews 13:4

instituted by God—Genesis 2:18-24

our marriage with God—Isaiah 54:5; Hosea 2:16,19,20; Ephesians 5:22-33

MATERIALISM (see also SELFISHNESS)

warnings against—Proverbs 23:4,5; Ecclesiastes 4:4; 5:8— 6:12; Matthew 6:19-21,24-33; 16:26; 19:21,22,24; Luke 12:15; 1 John 2:15; Psalm 49:16-20

contentment urged—Proverbs 30:8,9; 1 Timothy 6:6-10,17

MONEY (see MATERIALISM, STEWARDSHIP)

OBEDIENCE

of children—Ephesians 6:1-3; Colossians 3:20

toward God—John 14:15; 1 John 2:3; 5:3

toward leaders—Romans 13:1-7; Hebrews 13:17

PARENTS

responsibility of—Ephesians 6:4; Colossians 3:21

care for—Proverbs 23:22; 1 Timothy 5:4

relationship after marriage—Genesis 2:24

PATIENCE

with God—Psalm 37:7,8; Lamentations 3:26,27

with suffering—Romans 12:12; James 5:7-11

fruit of the Spirit—Galatians 5:22

with others—1 Thessalonians 5:14

God's patience with the sinner—2 Peter 3:9

PEER PRESSURE

warnings against—Proverbs 1:10; Luke 12:4-9

examples of—Matthew 26:69-75; 27:11-26

solution—Romans 12:2

PERSEVERANCE

in suffering—2 Corinthians 4:8-11; 12:7-10; James 1:2-4,12

of apostle Paul—2 Corinthians 11:23-27

in the faith—Matthew 24:13; 1 Corinthians 15:58; 16:13;
    Galatians 6:9; Revelation 2:10

from God—Isaiah 40:30,31

PRAYER

power of—James 5:16

from the heart—Psalm 119:145; Matthew 6:7; 15:8

pray with confidence—Mark 11:24; James 1:6,7

privilege we have through Christ—Psalm 143:1,2;
    John 16:23

ROMANTIC LOVE

see Song of Songs, esp. 4:1-7; 5:10-16

SELF-ESTEEM

of sinner—Luke 15:21; Romans 3:12; 7:18

of Christian—Luke 18:9-14; Philippians 3:4-11; 1 Peter 2:9;
    Luke 12:6,7

SELFISHNESS (see also MATERIALISM)

condemned—Proverbs 15:27; 2 Timothy 3:2

consideration encouraged—Romans 15:2;
1 Corinthians 10:24; Philippians 2:3,4

live for Christ—2 Corinthians 5:15; Philippians 1:21

SEXUAL INTERCOURSE

blessing of marriage—Genesis 2:24; 1 Corinthians 7:3-5

as a union—Genesis 2:24; 1 Corinthians 6:16

forbidden outside of marriage—1 Corinthians 6:9,10;
Hebrews 13:4

SEXUAL BEAUTY (see ROMANTIC LOVE)

SIBLING RIVALRY

examples of—Genesis 4:1-12; Genesis 27; 37

dealing with—see ENDURANCE, PATIENCE, PERSEVER-
ANCE, DISCIPLINE, AND AGING

SPIRITUAL GROWTH

father as leader—Ephesians 6:4

husband as leader—Ephesians 5:22-33

essential part of Christian life—1 Peter 2:2; 2 Peter 3:18

STEWARDSHIP

motivation—2 Corinthians 5:14; 8:9

principles—Proverbs 3:9; 23:26; Matthew 6:33; Acts 20:35;
Romans 12:1,6-8; 1 Corinthians 10:31; 12:12-31; 16:2;
2 Corinthians 8:1—9:15; 1 Peter 4:10,11

SUBMISSION

of all—Ephesians 5:21

of the wife—Ephesians 5:22-24; Titus 2:4,5; 1 Peter 3:1-6

TRUST (see also JEALOUSY)

in the Lord—Psalm 37:5; Proverbs 3:5; Isaiah 26:4;
John 14:1

one another—1 Corinthians 13:4-7

WEALTH (see STEWARDSHIP, MATERIALISM)

WIFE

qualities of good wife—Proverbs 31:10-31; 1 Peter 3:1-7

role of—Genesis 2:18; Ephesians 5:22-24

cherished—Ephesians 5:25-33; Colossians 3:19; 1 Peter 3:7

WOMAN—Role of Man and Woman

roles set up at Creation—Genesis 2:18-24

roles affected by sin—Genesis 3:16-19

God's will for all—1 Timothy 2:11-15

sexes equal before God—Galatians 3:26-28

applied to church—1 Corinthians 11:3-16; 14:33-35

applied to marriage—Ephesians 5:22-24